W9-BKD-743

by Harry Patterson

RED-LETTER PRESS, INC.

THE FOOTBALL WIZ TRIVIA QUIZ

ISBN: 0-940462-53-2

Printed in the United States of America

For information address:

Red-Letter Press, Inc.
P.O. Box 393, Saddle River, NJ 07458

Acknowledgments

Cover design and typography: s.w.artz, inc.

Editorial: Ellen Fischbein

Contributors: Angela Demers
Jack Kreismer
Jim Tomlinson

Jaguar
Bowl Jaguar
Bowl Bears Ravens
Dolphins Packers Saints Cotton
Chargers Jets Bucs Orange Bowl 49ers
s Falcons Fiesta Bowl Cowboys Colts
Cotton Bowl Browns Raiders Eagles Vi
e Bowl 49ers Steelers Seahawks Tita
Bowl Cowboys Colts NFL Bengals Pa
Raiders Eagles Vikings Patriots Super B
Seahawks Titans Cardinals Bills Suga
Bengals Panthers Rose Bowl Giants Ch
s Super Bowl Jaguars Rams Redskin
e Bowl Bears Ravens NCAA Broncos
Chiefs Dolphins Packers Saints Cotton
Redskins Chargers Jets Bucs Orange Bow
AA Broncos Falcons Fiesta Bowl Cow
Saints Cotton Bowl Browns Raiders
ucs Orange Bowl 49ers Steelers Sea
Fiesta Bowl Cowboys Colts NFL B
Raiders Eagles Vikings Patriot
wks Titans Cardinals
ers Rose Bowl Ra

SPECIAL THANKS TO:

Dave Dunkle

Dave Smith

Gennie Goforth

The Staff at the Shaler North Hills Library

The Gang at the Shaler Lounge

The Gang at the River City Inn

thers
owl Jaguars
owl Bears Ravens
hins Packers Saints Cotton
rgers Jets Bucs Orange Bowl 49ers
Falcons Fiesta Bowl Cowboys Colts
otton Bowl Browns Raiders Eagles Vi
Bowl 49ers Steelers Seahawks Tita
owl Cowboys Colts NFL Bengals Pa
ders Eagles Vikings Patriots Super B
eahawks Titans Cardinals Bills Suga
engals Panthers Rose Bowl Giants Ch
ts Super Bowl Jaguars Rams Redskin
Bowl Bears Ravens NCAA Broncos
hiefs Dolphins Packers Saints Cotton
skins Chargers Jets Bucs Orange Bow
AA Broncos Falcons Fiesta Bowl Cow
Saints Cotton Bowl Browns Raiders Sea
ucs Orange Bowl 49ers Steelers NFL B
Fiesta Bowl Cowboys Colts Patriot
Raiders Eagles Vikings Cardinals
ks Titans Rose Bowl
ers Ram

Introduction

Red-Letter Press proudly kicks off *The Football Wiz Trivia Quiz.* Formatted in ten-question quizzes, it features an all-star selection of pigskin puzzlers.

Harry Patterson brings you a book interspersed with quips and quotes and loaded with trivia ... Who retired from football at 27 as one of the game's top defensive tackles to pursue a successful career as a Grammy-winning songwriter? ... Why was the 1942 Rose Bowl played in Durham, North Carolina? ... What was the price of the cheapest ticket to the first Super Bowl?

The answers are all inside. Now let's find out if you're a football wiz or wannabe.

Jack Kreismer
Publisher

nthers
Bowl Jaguars
Bowl Bears Ravens N
phins Packers Saints Cotton
rgers Jets Bucs Orange Bowl 49ers
s Falcons Fiesta Bowl Cowboys Colts
otton Bowl Browns Raiders Eagles V
e Bowl 49ers Steelers Seahawks Ti
Bowl Cowboys Colts NFL Bengals Pa
ders Eagles Vikings Patriots Super B
eahawks Titans Cardinals Bills Suga
engals Panthers Rose Bowl Giants Ch
ls Super Bowl Jaguars Rams Redski
r Bowl Bears Ravens NCAA Broncos
hiefs Dolphins Packers Saints Cotton
skins Chargers Jets Bucs Orange Bo
AA Broncos Falcons Fiesta Bowl Cow
Saints Cotton Bowl Browns Raiders
ucs Orange Bowl 49ers Steelers Sea
Fiesta Bowl Cowboys Colts NFL B
aiders Eagles Vikings Patrio
Titans Cardinals
Rose Bowl
Ra

The
FOOTBALL
WIZ
Trivia
QUIZ

thers
owl Jaguars Ravens N
owl Bears Saints Cotton
hins Packers Orange Bowl 49ers
gers Jets Bucs Cowboys Colts
Falcons Fiesta Bowl Eagles Vi
tton Bowl Browns Raiders Tita
Bowl 49ers Steelers Seahawks Pan
owl Cowboys Colts NFL Bengals Super B
lers Eagles Vikings Patriots Sugar
ahawks Titans Cardinals Bills Ch
ngals Panthers Rose Bowl Giants Redskin
Super Bowl Jaguars Rams Broncos
Bowl Bears Ravens NCAA Cotton
hiefs Dolphins Packers Saints Orange Bow
skins Chargers Jets Bucs Fiesta Bowl Cow
A Broncos Falcons Browns Raiders
Saints Cotton Bowl 49ers Steelers Seah
cs Orange Bowl Cowboys Colts NFL Be
Fiesta Bowl Eagles Vikings Patriot
aiders Titans Cardinals
ks Rose Bowl Ram

GETTING STARTED

What was the very first NFL (or AFL) team each of the following played for?

1. Jim Marshall
2. Nick Buoniconti
3. Jim Plunkett
4. Steve Young
5. George Blanda
6. Fran Tarkenton
7. Y.A. Tittle
8. Earl Morrall
9. Deion Sanders
10. Ted Hendricks

Sec. 82 Row E Seat 17

Enter Gate B

"We definitely will be improved this year. Last year we scheduled 10 games. This year we only scheduled nine."

–Montana State football coach Ray Jenkins

ANSWERS

1. Browns (1960)
2. Patriots (1962)
3. Patriots (1971)
4. Buccaneers (1985)
5. Bears (1949)
6. Vikings (1961)
7. Colts (1950)
8. 49ers (1956)
9. Falcons (1989)
10. Colts (1969)

FULL SEASON

Sec. 17 Row K Seat 22 Gate F

"Old place-kickers never die, they just go on missing the point."

–Lou "The Toe" Groza

DUOS

1. These Steelers backfield mates combined for over 10,000 rushing yards in the '70s.
2. Both had their careers somewhat shortened by injury, but the Bears hit the jackpot when they drafted these two future Hall of Famers in the first round in 1965.
3. The undefeated 1972 Dolphins featured these two backs who each rushed for 1,000 yards.
4. These two defensive players were the first Super Bowl co-MVPs.
5. Mark these two down as Dan Marino's favorite targets in the '80s.
6. They served as co-coaches of the Bears while George Halas served in the Navy.
7. These two quarterbacks led the Dolphins to a perfect season in 1972.
8. These Raider teammates formed one of the best cornerback tandems ever, from 1983-86.
9. Despite the fact that they played for the same team, these two quarterbacks were both among the top passers of 1951.
10. In his first year with the Eagles, Buddy Ryan played a mostly unsuccessful game of musical quarterbacks with these two snap takers.

ANSWERS

1. Franco Harris and Rocky Bleier
2. Gale Sayers and Dick Butkus
3. Larry Csonka and Mercury Morris
4. Harvey Martin and Randy White
5. Mark Clayton and Mark Duper
6. Hunk Anderson and Luke Johnsos
7. Bob Griese and Earl Morrall
8. Lester Hayes and Mike Haynes
9. Bob Waterfield and Norm Van Brocklin
10. Ron Jaworski and Randall Cunningham

Sec. 07
Row 19
Seat 12
Enter Gate C
Upper Tier

"Coach Lombardi is very fair. He treats us all like dogs."

–Green Bay lineman Henry Jordan

FULL SEASON TICKET

THREES

1. Which three NFL teams provided balance by jumping to the American Football Conference when the AFL and NFL merged in 1970?
2. Name the three quarterbacks chosen 1-2-3 in the 1999 NFL draft, the first time this happened since 1971.
3. Name the three from 1971.
4. Name the three Detroit Lions who each had over 100 receiving yards on Thanksgiving, 1995, against the Vikings as Scott Mitchell passed for 410 yards.
5. The broadcast crew for ABC's first Super Bowl telecast (XIX in 1985) consisted of Frank Gifford, Don Meredith and which then-still-active quarterback?
6. Name the "Three Amigos."
7. Which three NFL cities built multi-purpose, way-too-similar, now-obsolete "cookie-cutter" stadiums in the early '70s?
8. Which three Miami Dolphins jumped to the new World Football League, giving it a measure of credibility, at least initially?
9. In 1980 the "Air Coryell" Chargers became the first team to field three 1,000 yard receivers. Who were they?
10. This didn't happen again until the Redskins did it with Gary Clark, Art Monk and Ricky Sanders. Who was the Skins primary quarterback that season?

ANSWERS

1. The Steelers, Browns and Colts
2. Tim Couch, Donovan McNabb and Akili Smith
3. Jim Plunkett, Archie Manning and Dan Pastorini
4. Brad Perriman, Herman Moore and Johnnie Morton
5. Joe Theismann
6. Vance Johnson, Ricky Nattiel and Mark Jackson
7. Pittsburgh (Three Rivers Stadium), Philadelphia (Veteran's Stadium) and Cincinnati (Riverfront Stadium)
8. Larry Csonka, Paul Warfield and Jim Kiick
9. John Jefferson, Charlie Joiner and Kellen Winslow
10. Mark Rypien

"This job is better than I could get if I used my college degree, which, at this point, I can't remember what it was in."

–Pro tackle Bob Golic, after signing a new contract

Sec. 16
Row 51
Seat 7a
Enter Gate G
Lower Tier

TOUCHDOWN TOMES

Match each of the following books with the author (and in some cases the word "author" is used very loosely).

1. *I Can't Wait Until Tomorrow … 'Cause I Get Better Looking Every Day*
2. *Hey! Wait a Minute! I Wrote a Book!*
3. *Just Give Me the Damn Ball*
4. *My Life in Football, Television and Movies*
5. *Paper Lion* (basis for the movie)
6. *Quarterbacking*
7. *In the Trenches*
8. *Run to Daylight*
9. *Semi-Tough* (basis for the movie)
10. *North Dallas Forty* (basis for the movie)

A. Alex Karras
B. John Madden
C. Pete Gent
D. Dan Jenkins
E. George Plimpton
F. Vince Lombardi
G. Joe Namath
H. Keyshawn Johnson
I. Joe Theismann
J. Reggie White

"MRI, did I pronounce that right?"

–Former Tampa Bay Bucs coach Richard Williamson

ANSWERS

1. G
2. B
3. H
4. A
5. E
6. I
7. J
8. F
9. D
10. C

Sec. Row Seat
82 E 17
Enter Gate B

"If I drop dead tomorrow, at least I'll know I died in good health."

-Bum Phillips

MULTI-SPORT

1. Who was the long-time 49ers quarterback who also made a mark as a pro golfer, most notably on the Senior PGA Tour?
2. Who is the only man to play in a World Series and a Super Bowl?
3. Who was an outfielder for the New York Giants in 1944-45 and a halfback for the New York Giants in 1945-46?
4. Which Major League Baseball team drafted Dan Marino?
5. Which Major League Baseball team drafted John Elway?
6. Who hit a home run for the Yankees less than a week before his NFL debut?
7. Who played for the Pirates and the Steelers?
8. What Cleveland Browns Hall of Fame quarterback also played pro basketball?
9. Name the Minnesota Golden Gopher who was drafted by the NBA Atlanta Hawks, the ABA Utah Stars, the San Diego Padres and the Minnesota Vikings.
10. Who played briefly for the Yankees in 1919 before moving on to become a player/coach/owner/legend in the NFL?

ANSWERS

1. John Brodie
2. Deion Sanders
3. Steve "Flip" Filipowicz
4. Kansas City Royals
5. New York Yankees
6. Deion Sanders, in 1989
7. No, not the organist — Rex Johnston played several years in the minors before getting into a few games with the Pirates in 1964. In 1960 he made the Steelers as a halfback and was mainly used as a kick returner.
8. Otto Graham
9. Dave Winfield
10. George Halas

FULL SEASON

Sec. 17 Row K Seat 22 Gate F

"The Rose Bowl is the only bowl that I have ever seen that I didn't have to clean."

-Erma Bombeck

THE ONES THAT GOT AWAY

1. What Hall of Fame quarterback was drafted by the Steelers in 1955, cut in preseason and picked up by the Colts?
2. Jim Plunkett led the Raiders to two Super Bowl victories in the '80s after being cut by which team?
3. Which team drafted Bo Jackson first overall in 1986 but lost out when he initially chose to play baseball?
4. Which team left rookie quarterbacks Len Dawson and Jack Kemp on the bench in the late '50s prompting them to jump to other leagues?
5. The Tampa Bay Bucs chose Ricky Bell first overall in 1977. Who went next?
6. If the coin toss went the other way, which future Hall of Famer would the Bears have been able to draft in 1970?
7. Name the kicker, cut by the Bills in 1982, who was picked up by the Steelers and went on to become their all-time leading scorer.
8. Lyle Alzado got a ring with the Raiders for Super Bowl XVIII. Which team traded him straight up for an eighth-round draft choice the previous season?
9. Five quarterbacks were chosen before Dan Marino in the 1983 draft. How many can you name?
10. Joe Montana wasn't drafted until the last pick of the third round in 1979, but three quarterbacks were taken in the first round. Steve Fuller and Jack Thompson were two. The other was a future Super Bowl MVP. Who was he?

ANSWERS

1. Johnny Unitas
2. The San Francisco 49ers
3. The Tampa Bay Buccaneers
4. The Pittsburgh Steelers
5. Tony Dorsett, by the Cowboys
6. Terry Bradshaw
7. Gary Anderson
8. The Cleveland Browns
9. John Elway, Jim Kelly, Todd Blackledge, Tony Eason and Ken O'Brien
10. Phil Simms

Sec. 07
Row 19
Seat 12
Enter Gate C
Upper Tier

"Scheduling is very important, depending upon whom you play."

-Bo Schembechler

FULL SEASON TICKET

WHO YOU TALKIN' 'BOUT?

Below are ten quotes and the person quoted. Can you figure out who each was talking about?

1. "The boy is good. How many times can you say it?" *-Mark Clayton*
2. "He's great to the old guys. He's got one trainer just to treat varicose veins." *-Alex Karras*
3. "He's such a perfectionist that if he were married to Dolly Parton he'd expect her to cook." *-Don Meredith*
4. "[He] was famous for being associated with only one club all his life — the one he held over your head during salary talks." *-Bobby Layne*
5. "He'd-a lived a hell of a lot longer if he hadn't played Pittsburgh six times in two years." *-Bum Phillips* (prewriting an epitaph)
6. "He may not be in a class by himself, but whatever class he's in, it doesn't take long to call the roll." *-Bum Phillips*
7. "He's so dumb he can't spell 'cat' if you spotted him the 'c' and the 'a.'" *-Thomas Henderson*
8. "The shoulder surgery was a success. The lobotomy failed." *-Mike Ditka*
9. "[He] doesn't have many rules, but one of them is don't lose to the Cowboys." *-Mike Golic*
10. "He must shower in Vaseline." *-Lester Hayes*

ANSWERS

1. Dan Marino
2. George Allen
3. Tom Landry
4. George Halas
5. Himself
6. Earl Campbell
7. Terry Bradshaw
8. Jim McMahon
9. Buddy Ryan
10. Randall Cunningham

"If you're a pro coach, NFL stands for 'Not For Long.'"

-Jerry Glanville

Sec. 16
Row 51
Seat 7a
Enter Gate G
Lower Tier

"THE" NICKNAMES

Name the football figure known by each of "the" following nicknames.

1. The Bus
2. The Toe
3. The Refrigerator
4. The Kansas Comet
5. The Horse
6. The Steamer
7. The Snake
8. The Tooz
9. The Manster
10. The King

Sec. 82 Row E Seat 17
Enter Gate B

"I had the air-conditioning at my back."

-Rusty Fricke, after kicking a 60-yard field goal in an Arena Football League game

ANSWERS

1. Jerome Bettis
2. Lou Groza
3. William Perry
4. Gale Sayers
5. Alan Ameche
6. Stanley Morgan
7. Ken Stabler
8. John Matuszak
9. Randy White
10. Hugh McElhenny

FULL SEASON

Sec. 17 Row K Seat 22 Gate F

"I just hope I never get kicked in the groin."

-John Elway, after newspapers showed pictures of his torn biceps tendon

BOWLING YOU OVER

1. Two schools have won each of the five major bowl games — the Rose, Cotton, Sugar, Orange and Fiesta Bowls. Can you name either of them?
2. What was the Florida Citrus Bowl originally called?
3. In the last 25 years, only one school has gone undefeated and won back-to-back national championships. Name the team. (Hint: They won the Orange and Fiesta Bowls.)
4. Who is Charlie Bauman and why was Woodie Hayes mad at him, anyway?
5. What is the oldest college bowl game?
6. In what stadium is the Sugar Bowl played?
7. What is the NCAA Division III national championship game called?
8. True or false? No Ivy League school has played in a major college football game.
9. What is the name of the college bowl game played in San Diego's Qualcomm Stadium?
10. Why was the 1942 Rose Bowl played in Durham, North Carolina?

ANSWERS

1. Notre Dame and Penn State
2. The Tangerine Bowl
3. Nebraska, 1994-95
4. He's the Clemson defender the Ohio State coach punched after he had made a game-saving interception in the Gator Bowl, December 29, 1978.
5. The Rose Bowl — Michigan shut out Stanford, 49-0, on January 1, 1902.
6. The Superdome in New Orleans
7. The Amos Alonzo Stagg Bowl
8. False — But the last to play in one was Columbia University back in 1934 when they defeated Stanford, 7-0, in the Rose Bowl
9. The Holiday Bowl
10. Because of military conditions during World War II, the U.S. did not want large crowd gatherings on the West Coast. The only time the contest was not played in Pasadena, the game was moved to Durham where Duke was upset by Oregon State, 20-16.

PORTRAYALS

Match each of the following with the actor who portrayed him in either a theatrical or TV movie.

1.	Brian Piccolo	A.	Peter Berg
2.	Gale Sayers	B.	Mark Singer
3.	John Cappelletti	C.	James Caan
4.	George Halas	D.	Billy Dee Williams
5.	Dennis Byrd	E.	Jack Warden
6.	Rocky Bleier	F.	Charles Bickford
7.	Art Rooney	G.	Burt Lancaster
8.	George Plimpton	H.	Robert Urich
9.	Jim Thorpe	I.	Alan Alda
10.	Pop Warner	J.	Art Carney

Sec. 07
Row 19
Seat 12
Enter
Gate C
Upper Tier

"I don't like to look back in retrospect."

–Former NFL quarterback Vince Ferragamo

FULL SEASON TICKET

ANSWERS

1. C (*Brian's Song*, TV, 1971)
2. D (*Brian's Song*)
3. B (*Something For Joey*, TV, 1977)
4. E (*Brian's Song*)
5. A (*Rise and Walk*, TV, 1994)
6. H (*Fighting Back*, TV, 1980)
7. J (*Fighting Back*)
8. I (*Paper Lion*, 1968)
9. G (*Jim Thorpe–All American*, 1951)
10. F (*Jim Thorpe–All American*)

Sec. Row Seat
82 E 17
Enter Gate B

**"When you win you're an old pro.
When you lose, you're an old man."**

-Former NFL quarterback Charley Conerly

MELTING POT

Match each of the following with the country of his birth.

1. Ted Hendricks	A. New Zealand
2. Jan Stenerud	B. Guatamala
3. Gary Anderson (the kicker)	C. South Africa
4. Ernie Stautner	D. Mexico
5. Junior Seau	E. Norway
6. Tony Zendejas	F. Germany
7. Morten Andersen	G. Cyprus
8. Steve Christie	H. Canada
9. David Dixon	I. Denmark
10. Garo Yepremian	J. U.S.A.

"I'd just like to put it behind me."

–Tennessee quarterback Peyton Manning, when asked about the alleged "mooning" of a teammate in front of a female trainer

Sec. 16

Row 51

Seat 7a

Enter Gate G

Lower Tier

ANSWERS

1. B
2. E
3. C
4. F
5. J
6. D
7. I
8. H
9. A
10. G

FULL SEASON

Sec. 17 Row K Seat 22 Gate F

"I told them publicity is like poison ... it won't hurt you if you don't swallow it."

–*Joe Paterno*

TEAMS ON THE MOVE

1. They became the Chicago Bears in 1922. In what city and under what name were they founded in 1920?
2. The present day Washington Redskins began play in 1932 for which city?
3. What were the Redskins known as during their inaugural season?
4. Which franchise was virtually treated as an expansion team in 1996, but had actually played more than half a century in another city?
5. The St. Louis Rams won the Super Bowl in 2000, capping their fifth season in that city after moving from Los Angeles. From what city did they move to L.A. in 1946?
6. Despite moving more than 1,200 miles west in 1988 the Cardinals still played in which division?
7. What unusual "move" took place between the Rams and the Colts in 1972?
8. What was the first franchise to win Super Bowls for two different cities?
9. What were the Cardinals known as from 1988-93?
10. The Oilers became the Titans in 1999. Which current NFL team was previously known as the Titans?

ANSWERS

1. The Decatur Staleys
2. Boston
3. The Boston Braves
4. The Baltimore Ravens (previously the Cleveland Browns)
5. Cleveland
6. NFC East
7. The owners moved but the teams stayed (for the time being anyhow) as Robert Irsay's L.A. Rams were swapped for Carroll Rosenbloom's Baltimore Colts.
8. The Raiders, for Oakland in 1997 and 1981 and for L.A. in 1984
9. The Phoenix Cardinals
10. The Jets, in the AFL from 1960-62

Sec. Row Seat
82 E 17
Enter Gate B

"You guys line up alphabetically by height."

–Florida State coach Bill Peterson

AGES FOR THE AGES

Within a year either way, how old was …

1. George Halas when he coached his final game?
2. Joe Namath when he led the Jets to victory in Super Bowl III?
3. Brian Piccolo when he died of cancer?
4. Gale Sayers when he played his final game?
5. George Blanda when he played his final game?
6. William Perry when he scored a touchdown in Super Bowl XX?
7. Doug Flutie when he returned to the NFL with the Bills?
8. Joe Montana when he threw his final pass?
9. Howard Cosell when he did his final *Monday Night Football* broadcast?
10. Bronko Nagurski when he returned to the Bears for one more season after a five year absence to help the team during the World War II manpower shortage?

Sec. 07

Row 19

Seat 12

Enter
Gate C
Upper Tier

"Baseball is what we were.
Football is what we've become."

-Mary McGrory, columnist

FULL SEASON TICKET

ANSWERS

1. 72
2. 25
3. 26
4. 28
5. 48
6. 23
7. 35
8. 38
9. 63
10. 34

"The thing I like about football is that you don't have to take a shower before you go to work."

-Jay Hilgenberg

Sec. 16

Row 51

Seat 7a

Enter Gate G

Lower Tier

MNF

1. What year and on which network did *Monday Night Football* debut?
2. Who were the original three *MNF* announcers?
3. If *MNF* is considered as a network prime time program, what was the only other network prime time program on the air longer at the beginning of the 2000 season?
4. Name the producer of *MNF* during the glory years of 1972-77 who returned to the post for the 2000 season.
5. Within one either way, for how many seasons was Howard Cosell in the *MNF* booth?
6. Name the ex-jock who replaced Don Meredith in 1974 but didn't make it past the exhibition season.
7. Millions of Americans first learned of what tragic news event from Howard Cosell late in a *MNF* broadcast on December 8, 1980?
8. Don Meredith pulled two stints on *MNF*. Which was longer, the first or second?
9. Which broadcaster was voted into the Hall of Fame in 1977, during his tenure with *MNF*?
10. What comedian was given the A OK in Y2K to join the *MNF* broadcast crew?

ANSWERS

1. In 1970 on ABC
2. Howard Cosell, Don Meredith and Keith Jackson
3. *60 Minutes*, which debuted in 1968
4. Don Ohlmeyer
5. 14
6. Fred Williamson
7. The death of John Lennon
8. The second — He did the first four seasons and returned for the 1977-84 seasons.
9. Frank Gifford
10. Dennis Miller

FULL SEASON Sec. 17 Row K Seat 22 Gate F

"No, thank you. I'm trying to quit."

-Packers quarterback Brett Favre, declining make-up powder before a TV interview with ABC's Al Michaels

WHO 'DAT?

1. He was the first tight end inducted into the Hall of Fame.
2. He's the first left-handed quarterback to win a Super Bowl.
3. Of the top 20 all-time leading rushers he is the only one with an average yards-per-carry over 5.0.
4. In 1980 he had four games in which he rushed for over 200 yards.
5. He has been sacked more times than any quarterback in NFL history.
6. He retired in 1962 as the last of the two-way starters.
7. He sat out the 1961 season with a head injury but returned in 1962 to play three more seasons capping a Hall of Fame career for the Giants.
8. He was the only man to lead the NFL in rushing yards for the season while Jim Brown was active.
9. He was the linchpin in the largest trade in NFL history, going from the Cowboys to the Vikings in a transaction involving 18 players or draft choices.
10. He was the first Super Bowl MVP not named Bart Starr.

ANSWERS

1. Mike Ditka
2. Ken Stabler
3. Jim Brown with 5.2
4. Earl Campbell
5. John Elway
6. Chuck Bednarik as Eagles center and linebacker
7. Frank Gifford
8. Jim Taylor, Packers in 1963
9. Herschel Walker
10. Joe Namath in Super Bowl III — Starr won in I and II.

Sec. 07
Row 19
Seat 12
Enter Gate C
Upper Tier

"It is so quiet, you could hear a sweat sock drop."

–Buffalo coach Marv Levy, on the Bills' locker room after losing in Super Bowl XXVI

FULL SEASON TICKET

HOMETOWN HEROES

Match each of the following with his birthplace.

1. Lyle Alzado	A. Starkville, Mississippi
2. Jim Brown	B. St. Simons, Georgia
3. Terry Bradshaw	C. Salt Lake City, Utah
4. John Brodie	D. Beaver Falls, Pennsylvania
5. Dick Butkus	E. Brooklyn, New York
6. Jerry Rice	F. San Francisco, California
7. Gale Sayers	G. Shreveport, Louisiana
8. Emmitt Smith	H. Chicago, Illinois
9. Joe Namath	I. Pensacola, Florida
10. Steve Young	J. Wichita, Kansas

Sec. 82 Row E Seat 17

Enter Gate B

"Maybe I lost a step, but I had a few to lose."

–Veteran wide receiver Roy Green

ANSWERS

1. E
2. B
3. G
4. F
5. H
6. A
7. J
8. I
9. D
10. C

"It was like the pope not being allowed to say Mass."

–Bills linebacker Chris Spielman, on not working out for an extensive time because of a neck injury

Sec. 16

Row 51

Seat 7a

Enter Gate G

Lower Tier

BY ANY OTHER NAME

The following are not generally known by their given first names which are provided in the clues. Can you identify them by their more familiar names?

1. Sharmon was the first Dolphin to rush for 1,000 yards in a season since Larry Csonka and Mercury Morris.
2. Tiaini was All-America at USC and was a first-round draft choice for the Chargers.
3. Eugene rushed for exactly 1,000 yards in 1972.
4. Army fullback Felix was drafted in the first round by the Steelers but never played in the NFL.
5. Yelberton replaced Charlie Conerly late in the '61 season and led his team to the first of three consecutive conference championships.
6. Charles was Chuck Noll's very first draft choice with the Steelers.
7. Carlton was the first rusher in AFL history to reach 1,000 yards in a season.
8. Harold gave professional football instant credibility when he joined the Bears in 1925.
9. Grambling coach Eddie Robinson called Junious "the finest lineman I have seen."
10. The Steelers' Byron racked up more rushing yards than the Cowboys' Emmitt Smith in a losing cause in Super Bowl XXX.

ANSWERS

1. Karim Abdul-Jabbar, in 1996
2. Junior Seau
3. Mercury Morris
4. Doc Blanchard
5. Y.A. Tittle
6. Joe Greene
7. Cookie Gilchrist, Bills, 1962
8. Red Grange
9. Buck Buchanan
10. Bam Morris

FULL SEASON

Sec. 17 Row K Seat 22 Gate F

"I've only got two words: It ain't no surprise."

-Broncos cornerback Darrien Gordon, after an upset Super Bowl win over Green Bay

SEASONS TO REMEMBER

1. The Dolphins completed a perfect season with Super Bowl VII, yet went into the game as slight underdogs to which opponent?
2. The 49ers went 15-1 in 1984, losing only to whom?
3. The Bears went 15-1 in 1985, losing only to whom?
4. The Vikings went 15-1 in 1998, losing only to whom?
5. In the strike-shortened 1982 season the Redskins went 8-1, losing only to whom?
6. Of the teams cited in the previous four questions, which is the only one that did not go on to win the Super Bowl?
7. George Halas left for the Navy in October, but the Bears finished the 1942 regular season, 11-0. Who beat them for the championship?
8. Which team was AFC champion for four consecutive seasons yet never followed up with a Super Bowl win?
9. Which wild card team was dubbed the "Road Warriors" after winning three consecutive road games enroute to Super Bowl XX?
10. Which team went 13-0 in 1934, only to lose the championship to the Giants?

ANSWERS

1. The Redskins
2. The Steelers
3. The Dolphins
4. The Buccaneers
5. The Cowboys
6. The Vikings
7. The Redskins
8. The Bills
9. The Patriots
10. The Bears

"You have to understand Thurman. If you didn't know him, you'd think he was an idiot. We've known him two or three years now, and we know he's an idiot."

–Will Wolford, on Bills teammate Thurman Thomas

Sec. 16
Row 51
Seat 7a
Enter Gate G
Lower Tier

INTIMIDATORS

Match 'em up.

1. Sack Exchange (defensive line)	A. '80s Dolphins
2. Steel Curtain (defense)	B. '70s Vikings
3. Hogs (offensive line)	C. '60s/'70s Cowboys
4. Fearsome Foursome (defensive line)	D. '50s 49ers
5. Doomsday Defense	E. '70s Dolphins
6. Million Dollar Backfield	F. '60s Rams
7. No-Name Defense	G. '80s Redskins
8. Purple People Eaters (defense)	H. '70s Steelers
9. Killer B's (defense)	I. '80s/'90s Broncos
10. Three Amigos (receivers)	J. '80s Jets

Sec. 07
Row 19
Seat 12
Enter
Gate C
Upper Tier

"If you see a defensive team with dirt and mud on their backs, they've had a bad day."

-John Madden

FULL SEASON TICKET

ANSWERS

1. J
2. H
3. G
4. F
5. C
6. D
7. E
8. B
9. A
10. I

Sec. 82 Row E Seat 17

Enter Gate B

"Place-kickers aren't football players. They're hired feet."

-Alex Karras

PRIZE PACKAGES

1. Who's the only two-time Heisman trophy winner?
2. Who gets the Harlon Hill Trophy?
3. The Outland trophy goes to the top interior lineman. The winner of the 1996 award became the NFL's number one draft pick the next year. Who is it?
4. What two Big Ten teams play annually for the Little Brown Jug?
5. Iowa's football stadium was named for a former Heisman Trophy recipient. Can you name it?
6. What Heisman Trophy winner became an NBA player?
7. The Butkus Award, given to the top collegiate linebacker, was introduced in 1985. What player, later a bust in the pros, won the award the first two years?
8. Indiana and Purdue play for what prize every year?
9. In 1916, Georgia Tech clobbered Cumberland College, 222-0 in college football's most lopsided score in history. Who was Georgia Tech's coach? (Hint: Remember the category.)
10. Who is the only man to win an Olympic gold medal, play in a baseball World Series and be elected to both the College and Pro Football Halls of Fame?

ANSWERS

1. Archie Griffin of Ohio State, 1974 and '75
2. The nation's outstanding NCAA Division II player
3. Orlando Pace
4. Michigan and Minnesota
5. (Nile) Kinnick Stadium
6. Charlie Ward of Florida State
7. Brian Bosworth
8. The Old Oaken Bucket
9. John Heisman – for whom the trophy was named
10. Jim Thorpe

Sec. 07
Row 19
Seat 12
Enter
Gate C
Upper Tier

"If my quarterback runs, I'll shoot him."

–Bill Parcells, on the run & shoot offense

FULL SEASON TICKET

WHAT'S THE SCORE?

Below are ten of the more memorable Super Bowls and the teams involved. Can you match each with its final score?

1. Super Bowl I — Packers over Chiefs	A. 34-19
2. Super Bowl III — Jets over Colts	B. 55-10
3. Super Bowl IX — Steelers over Vikings	C. 16-6
4. Super Bowl XIII — Steelers over Cowboys	D. 35-31
5. Super Bowl XXXIV — Rams over Titans	E. 16-7
6. Super Bowl XX — Bears over Patriots	F. 35-10
7. Super Bowl XXIV — 49ers over Broncos	G. 14-7
8. Super Bowl XXXIII — Broncos over Falcons	H. 27-17
9. Super Bowl XXX — Cowboys over Steelers	I. 46-10
10. Super Bowl VII — Dolphins over Redskins	J. 23-16

FULL SEASON

Sec. 17 Row K Seat 22 Gate F

"The average football fan is a college graduate with an eighth grade education."

-Humorist Andy Rooney

ANSWERS

1. F
2. E
3. C
4. D
5. J
6. I
7. B
8. A
9. H
10. G

"He's the kind of guy that would steal a guy's eyeballs and then tell him he looks better without them."

–Former NFL coach Sam Rutigliano, on Raiders owner Al Davis

Sec. 16

Row 51

Seat 7a

Enter Gate G

Lower Tier

MONIKERS

Identify the football figures known by each of the following nicknames.

1. Sweetness
2. Slash
3. Whizzer
4. Crazylegs
5. Big Daddy
6. Fatso
7. Ironhead
8. Papa Bear
9. Prime Time
10. White Shoes

Sec. 82 Row E Seat 17

Enter Gate B

"Nobody in football should be called a genius. A genius is a guy like Norman Einstein."

-Joe Theismann

ANSWERS

1. Walter Payton
2. Kordell Stewart
3. Byron White
4. Elroy Hirsch
5. Eugene Lipscomb
6. Art Donovan
7. Craig Heyward
8. George Halas
9. Deion Sanders
10. Billy Johnson

FULL SEASON

Sec. 17 Row K Seat 22 Gate F

"I'm waiting for the day we see the 'wave' at the Metropolitan Opera."

–"Monday Night Football" announcer Al Michaels

BROKEN RECORDS

1. When Emmitt Smith scored 25 touchdowns in 1995, whose single-season record of 24 did he break?
2. In 1985, Bears kicker Kevin Butler set a rookie record for points scored with 144, breaking the record of 132 set in 1965 by whom? (Hint: He wasn't a kicker.)
3. In 1995, Jackie Slater played his 20th season with the Rams eclipsing the record of 19 seasons with one team held by whom?
4. In 1979, Dan Fouts passed for 4,087 yards, breaking the record of 4,007 held by whom?
5. Which running back would more than likely have become the leading rusher of all time if he had played in 1999?
6. Whose long-standing record for rushing touchdowns by a quarterback (40) was broken by Steve Young who retired with 43?
7. John Riggins gained 166 yards in Super Bowl XVII, breaking whose record of 158?
8. Which L.A. Raider broke Riggins' record the following year?
9. Don Shula's 317th career-coaching victory put him ahead of which legend on the all-time list?
10. Who was the first to pass Jim Brown on the all-time rushing yards list?

ANSWERS

1. John Riggins, 1983
2. Gale Sayers
3. Jim Marshall, Vikings
4. Joe Namath, 1967 in a 14-game season
5. Barry Sanders
6. Jack Kemp
7. Franco Harris, in Super Bowl IX
8. Marcus Allen, with 191
9. George Halas
10. Walter Payton

"I've got to wear more sun block."

–Former New York Giants quarterback Dave Brown, when asked what experience he'd gained from sitting out a preseason game on the sidelines

Sec. 16

Row 51

Seat 7a

Enter Gate G

Lower Tier

ALMA MATERS

Match each of the following with the school where he played college ball.

1. William Perry	A. Florida
2. Brett Favre	B. Brigham Young
3. Red Grange	C. Georgia
4. Herschel Walker	D. Southern Mississippi
5. Franco Harris	E. Illinois
6. Jim McMahon	F. Clemson
7. Joe Montana	G. Penn State
8. Emmitt Smith	H. Notre Dame
9. Barry Sanders	I. Pitt
10. Tony Dorsett	J. Oklahoma State

Sec. 07
Row 19
Seat 12
Enter Gate C
Upper Tier

"Football is, after all, a wonderful way to get rid of aggression without going to jail for it."

–Heywood Hale Broun

FULL SEASON TICKET

ANSWERS

1. F
2. D
3. E
4. C
5. G
6. B
7. H
8. A
9. J
10. I

Sec. Row Seat
82 E 17
Enter Gate B

"Anthony's only negative is that he has no negatives."

–Line coach Jim McNally, on the Cincinnati Bengals star offensive lineman Anthony Munoz

FOOTBALL FLICKS

1. What was Burt Reynolds' uniform number in both *The Longest Yard* and *Semi-Tough*?
2. The 1977 thriller *Black Sunday* incorporated actual footage from which Super Bowl?
3. Which two teams met in a fictional Super Bowl at the end of *Heaven Can Wait* before meeting for real in Super Bowl XIV?
4. Which 1976 action flick featured Merv Griffin singing the national anthem at a generic "championship" game because *Black Sunday* had previously nailed down the rights to using the Super Bowl as a backdrop?
5. Jimmy Johnson and Bill Cowher had cameos in which 1998 goofball comedy?
6. Which football legend played a fictionalized version of himself in 1931's *The Galloping Ghost*?
7. What was the name of the fictional yet somehow familiar pro team that Nick Nolte's character played for in *North Dallas Forty*?
8. Name the 1999 drama that purported to be a realistic look at pro football yet used all fictional teams because it wasn't sanctioned by the NFL.
9. Who played a washed-up New Orleans Saints quarterback in the 1969 drama *Number One*?
10. Dan Marino and the Miami Dolphins figured prominently in which 1994 comedy?

ANSWERS

1. #22
2. Super Bowl X, with the Steelers and the Cowboys
3. The Steelers and the Rams
4. *Two Minute Warning*
5. *The Waterboy*
6. Red Grange
7. The North Dallas Bulls
8. *Any Given Sunday*
9. Charlton Heston
10. *Ace Ventura: Pet Detective*

Sec. 07
Row 19
Seat 12
Enter Gate C
Upper Tier

"Actually I was only at Iowa two terms — Truman's and Eisenhower's."

–Former Detroit Lion and broadcaster Alex Karras

FULL SEASON TICKET

A SIMPLE YES OR NO WILL DO

1. Did Ed "Too Tall" Jones ever play for Jimmy Johnson with the Cowboys?
2. Was Joe Namath ever a *Monday Night Football* broadcaster?
3. Did Tony Dorsett get into the Hall of Fame before Earl Campbell?
4. Is Alex Karras in the Hall of Fame?
5. Is Jim Thorpe in the Hall of Fame?
6. Did the Steelers ever play a Super Bowl in a domed stadium?
7. Did Red Grange live into the 1990s?
8. Does George Halas hold any NFL records as player?
9. Did Kurt Warner ever start an NFL game prior to the 1999 season?
10. Did Vince Lombardi really say, "Winning isn't everything, it's the only thing"?

FULL SEASON

Sec. 17 Row K Seat 22 Gate F

"The first word you see in every airport is terminal."

-ESPN analyst Beano Cook, on his fear of flying

ANSWERS

1. Yes — They overlapped in 1989.
2. Yes, in 1985
3. No — Campbell entered in 1991, Dorsett in 1994.
4. No
5. Yes — He was a charter member in 1963.
6. No
7. Yes — He died in 1991 at the age of 87.
8. No, but he did until 1972 — The record, longest run with an opponent's fumble (98 yards), was set in 1923 against the Oorang Indians at Wrigley Field. It remains a Bears team record. By the way, the fumbler was Jim Thorpe.
9. No, but he did get into the last game of the 1998 season in the fourth quarter
10. No — It was actually said by John Wayne as a football coach in the 1953 movie *Trouble Along the Way*.

"Really, I never tuteled that boy."

-Former NFL coach Bum Phillips, asked if tutelage was a factor in his son, Wade, being named a pro head coach

QUOTABLES

Match each of the following quotes with the one who said it.

1. "In 26 years in the pros, I haven't noticed many changes. The players are faster, bigger, smarter and more disloyal to the owners. That's about it."
2. "There's nothing wrong with reading the game plan by the light of the juke box."
3. "Never worry about missing a field goal. Just blame the holder and think about kicking the next one."
4. "I love football. I really love football. As far as I'm concerned it's the second best thing in the world."
5. "Even when I was little I was big."
6. "It's not whether you get knocked down, it's whether you get up."
7. "If you can accept defeat and open your pay envelope without feeling guilty, you're stealing."
8. On the Super Bowl, "If it's the ultimate game, how come they're playing it again next year?"
9. "I'm not cocky, I'm confident. You know, there's a difference."
10. "The depth of anguish I felt after every loss the past few years has begun to reach an intensity that the thrill of victory can't overcome."

A. Keyshawn Johnson
B. Marv Levy
C. Joe Namath
D. Lou Groza
E. Ken Stabler
F. George Blanda
G. Duane Thomas
H. Vince Lombardi
I. William Perry
J. George Allen

ANSWERS

1. F
2. E
3. D
4. C
5. I
6. H
7. J
8. G
9. A
10. B

"A hotel operator called and said I had been indicted. I panicked and said, 'For what?'"

-John Mackey, on notification of his "induction" to the Pro Football Hall of Fame

Sec. 16

Row 51

Seat 7a

Enter Gate G

Lower Tier

COLLEGE CORNUCOPIA

1. Who holds the NCAA all-time rushing record for most yards gained during a career?
2. What legendary coach is credited with saying, "A tie is like kissing your sister"?
3. What did New York sculptor Frank Eliscu design?
4. Only three players had led the NCAA in rushing and then led the NFL in rushing the following year. Can you name any of them?
5. Which college team holds the record for most consecutive wins?
6. Who is the only college coach to have won more than 400 games?
7. What college player was the last overall NFL number-one pick in the 20th century?
8. As a freshman at the University of Georgia, I was third in Heisman Trophy voting. As a sophomore, I was second. In my junior year, I won the trophy. Who am I?
9. What's the score of a forfeited college football game?
10. What former Florida State running back starred in the movie *The Longest Yard*?

ANSWERS

1. Ron Dayne
2. Paul Bear Bryant
3. The Heisman Trophy
4. George Rogers, in 1981; Earl Campbell, 1978; and Byron White, 1938
5. The Oklahoma Sooners, coached by Bud Wilkinson, won 47 straight games from 1953-57.
6. Eddie Robinson
7. Penn State defensive end Courtney Brown, by the Cleveland Browns in 2000
8. Herschel Walker
9. 1-0
10. Burt Reynolds

FULL SEASON

Sec. 17 Row K Seat 22 Gate F

"I don't care what the tapes say, I didn't say it."

-L.A. Rams coach Ray Malavasi

SUPER NUMERALS

1. Which was the first Super Bowl to have the words "Super Bowl" on the ticket?
2. What was it officially called before that?
3. What did the cheapest ticket to the first Super Bowl go for?
4. What was the first Super Bowl to charge $100 for a ticket?
5. Who is credited with coming up with the name "Super Bowl"?
6. What facility was the first in a northern cold-weather city to host a Super Bowl?
7. Which team was the last "NFL Champion" not to win that distinction in a Super Bowl?
8. The first Super Bowl was simulcast by which two TV networks?
9. What was the first Super Bowl to officially use a Roman numeral?
10. Do the math. What year is Super Bowl L scheduled for?

ANSWERS

1. Super Bowl IV, 1970
2. AFL-NFL World Championship Game
3. $6 — $10 and $12 seats were also available if you wanted to splurge.
4. Super Bowl XXII, 1988
5. K.C. Chiefs owner Lamar Hunt
6. The Silverdome in Pontiac, Michigan for Super Bowl XVI in 1982
7. The Vikings, in 1969 — They went on to lose the Super Bowl to the AFL Chiefs. The two leagues merged into conferences the following season under the banner "NFL."
8. NBC and CBS
9. Super Bowl V, 1971
10. 2016 — Let's hope the Roman numeral thing is passé by then.

Sec. 07
Row 19
Seat 12
Enter Gate C
Upper Tier

"The greatest name in football."

-Alex Karras, on Cleveland Browns wide receiver Fair Hooker

FULL SEASON TICKET

REMEMBER THAT FABULOUS USFL

1. Who was the very first player drafted in the USFL (though he chose the NFL)?
2. Who was the owner of the New Jersey Generals?
3. For which team did Steve Young begin his pro career?
4. For which team did Jim Kelly begin his pro career?
5. Name the three consecutive Heisman Trophy winners who chose the USFL and the teams that signed them.
6. The USFL began play in 1983 with 12 franchises and added six more the following season. How many were left in 1986 when the league folded, canceling a proposed fall season?
7. The only sellout in USFL history was the Pittsburgh Maulers first home game, against the Birmingham Stallions. This was at least partly due to the fact the Stallions quarterback was which Pittsburgh boo-bird favorite?
8. Which team played in three cities for three owners with the same coach and most of the same players?
9. Name the future Super Bowl quarterback (and MVP) who took snaps for the Oklahoma/Arizona Wranglers.
10. Name the father who owned a USFL team and his son who owned an NFL team.

ANSWERS

1. Dan Marino
2. Donald Trump
3. L.A. Express
4. Houston Gamblers
5. Herschel Walker — Generals, Mike Rozier – Maulers, Doug Flutie — Generals
6. Eight
7. Former Steeler Cliff Stoudt
8. Boston/New Orleans/Portland Breakers
9. Doug Williams
10. Edward DeBartolo Sr. and Jr., Maulers and 49ers, respectively

"I think offensive linemen, in general, would be offended if you called them sophisticated."

–Cincinnati Bengals coach Dave Shula, when asked about the sophistication of his offensive line

Sec. 16
Row 51
Seat 7a
Enter Gate G
Lower Tier

PASSING FANCIES

1. Who was the first quarterback to pass for over 4,000 yards in a season?
2. Who was the first quarterback to pass for over 5,000 yards in a season?
3. Joe Montana completed 83 passes, 11 for touchdowns, in four Super Bowls. How many interceptions did he throw in those games?
4. The NFL record for touchdowns passes in a game is seven. Who threw six in a Super Bowl?
5. Which Super Bowl MVP completed an incredible 88% of his passes (22-25, 3 TDs)?
6. Who set a Super Bowl passing record with 414 yards?
7. Who retired, following the 1999 season, after completing more passes than any quarterback in NFL history?
8. Who is the only NFL quarterback to lead the league in single season passing yards both before and after the U.S. entered World War II?
9. Who set a record for single season passing yards in 1979, then proceeded to break his own record in each of the next two seasons?
10. Who retired following the 1999 season as the highest rated passer in NFL history?

ANSWERS

1. Joe Namath, with 4,007 in 1967, a 14-game season
2. Dan Marino, with 5,084 in 1984
3. None
4. Steve Young, in Super Bowl XXIX, 1995
5. Phil Simms, in Super Bowl XXI, 1987
6. Kurt Warner, in Super Bowl XXXIV, 2000
7. Dan Marino
8. Sammy Baugh, 1940 and 1947
9. Dan Fouts
10. Steve Young

Sec. Row Seat
82 E 17
Enter Gate B

"If I ever needed a brain transplant, I'd choose a sportswriter because I'd want a brain that had never been used."

-Norm Van Brocklin

MULTI-SPORT II

1. He was a defensive back with the Falcons for three seasons (1989-91) before moving on to a longer baseball career as an outfielder for the Cardinals and, later, the Braves.
2. His two-man bobsled team (with partner Brian Shimer) finished seventh in the 1992 Winter Olympics.
3. This well-known pro boxer faced off against Lyle Alzado in an exhibition bout in Denver in 1979.
4. He spent a mediocre season as a first baseman for the Washington Senators in 1963 before joining the Packers as a defensive back and punt returner the following year, later becoming the first Major League Baseball player to play in a Super Bowl.
5. Years before beginning an 18-season Hall of Fame coaching career he was a bench player for the 1950 NBA champion Minnesota Lakers.
6. This NFL head coach won three Super Bowls before retiring from football to become the owner of a NASCAR racing team.
7. He is the only man to serve as a Major League Baseball manager and an NFL head coach.
8. This future NFL Hall of Famer was All-America at Syracuse in both football and lacrosse.
9. He left the Cowboys in 1979 for an aborted boxing career, but returned the following year, better than ever, to play ten more seasons.
10. He left the Bears in 1937 for a more lucrative pro wrestling career.

ANSWERS

1. Brian Jordan
2. Herschel Walker
3. Muhammad Ali
4. Tom Brown
5. Bud Grant
6. Joe Gibbs
7. Hugo Bezdek, for the Pittsburgh Pirates in 1918-19 and the Cleveland Rams in 1937-38 — He also served a long stint as athletic director and head football coach at Penn State.
8. Jim Brown
9. Ed "Too Tall" Jones
10. Bronko Nagurski

FULL SEASON

Sec. 17 Row K Seat 22 Gate F

"Only when I look at you."

–Former quarterback Jim McMahon, responding to a reporter who'd asked if he felt any pain

IT'S ALL RELATIVE

1. Name the two brothers, both receivers/kick returners, who broke into the NFL in 1993. (Hint: The older brother previously played in Canada for two years.)
2. Name the father and son who combined for over 600 receptions, Dad for the Browns and his son for the Oilers and Cowboys.
3. Who were the father and son NFL head coaches who combined for 347 regular season career victories?
4. True or false? Quarterback Kurt Warner and former running back Curt (with a "C") Warner are brothers.
5. Which two brothers played on the Tampa Bay Bucs defense for the first five years of the team's existence?
6. Name the two kicking brothers who are both high on the NFL all-time scoring list.
7. Which NFL all-time great is the great-great-great grandson of Brigham Young?
8. Which Steelers division rival drafted Terry Bradshaw's younger brother Craig, also a quarterback, in 1980?
9. Center Bart Oates began a long pro career with the USFL Philadelphia Stars. Who was his older brother, also an offensive lineman, who ended his pro career with the same team after six NFL seasons?
10. Who began a 16-year Hall of Fame career with the 49ers the year after his older brother won an Olympic gold medal (decathlon) in Rome?

ANSWERS

1. Raghib and Qadry Ismail
2. Ray and Mike Renfro
3. Don and David Shula — Don won 328; David won 19.
4. False
5. Lee Roy and Dewey Selmon
6. Matt and Chris Bahr
7. Steve Young
8. Houston Oilers
9. Brad
10. Jimmy Johnson

Sec. 07
Row 19
Seat 12
Enter
Gate C
Upper Tier

"It's either a 30% cut or a 100% cut."

–Former Arizona Cardinals coach Buddy Ryan, on the salary options given to receiver Gary Clark

FULL SEASON TICKET

TURKEY TIME

1. Whom did the Detroit Lions host in their very first Thanksgiving game in 1934, kicking off a tradition that continues today?
2. Which team made 13 consecutive Thanksgiving trips to Detroit, 1951-63?
3. Name the Chicago Bear who returned an overtime opening kickoff 95 yards for a touchdown against the Lions on Thanksgiving, 1980, setting a record for the shortest overtime in history.
4. In only the second Detroit Thanksgiving overtime, the Lions beat which team following a controversial coin toss?
5. The Lion's most lopsided Thanksgiving victory (45-3) came in 1983 against which heavily-favored opponent?
6. Which defending NFL champ took a 10-0 record to Detroit on Thanksgiving only to lose their only game of the season as their quarterback was sacked 11 times?
7. Did the AFL hold any Thanksgiving games before the merger?
8. When did the Dallas Cowboys begin hosting Thanksgiving games — in 1966, 1972 or 1980?
9. Name the only other NFL team since the AFL merger to host a Thanksgiving game.
10. Where did the Lions play their Turkey Day games preceding the Pontiac Silverdome? And how about the Cowboys before Texas Stadium?

ANSWERS

1. The Bears — They lost 19-16.
2. The Packers
3. David Williams
4. The Steelers in 1998
5. The Steelers
6. Bart Starr and the Packers in 1962
7. Yes — one game from 1960-66 and two from 1967-70, with the teams rotating
8. 1966
9. The St. Louis Cardinals, instead of the Cowboys, in 1975 and 1977
10. The Lions played at Tiger Stadium; the Cowboys at the Cotton Bowl.

Sec. 82 Row E Seat 17

Enter Gate B

"His problem was that he couldn't win on the road."

-Buffalo Bills coach Marv Levy, on why Adolf Hitler was drubbed in Russia

"THE" NICKNAMES II

Again, name the football figure known by each of "the" following nicknames.

1. The Mad Duck
2. The Mad Stork
3. The Chief
4. The Dutchman
5. The Galloping Ghost
6. The Texas Tornado
7. The Minister of Defense
8. The Hammer
9. The Jet
10. The Tyler Rose

FULL SEASON

Sec. 17 Row K Seat 22 Gate F

"It's a lonesome walk to the sidelines, especially when thousands of people are cheering your replacement."

-Fran Tarkenton

ANSWERS

1. Alex Karras
2. Ted Hendricks
3. Art Rooney
4. Norm Van Brocklin
5. Red Grange
6. Sammy Baugh
7. Reggie White
8. Fred Williamson
9. Joe Perry
10. Earl Campbell

"I work out of my apartment. I'm like a hooker, except I work with my clothes on and I pay taxes."

–College football analyst Beano Cook

Sec. 16
Row 51
Seat 7a
Enter Gate G
Lower Tier

COACHING CAROUSEL

Each of the following head coaches led more than one team. Name the NFL (or AFL) teams they piloted.

1. Curly Lambeau — three teams
2. Vince Lombardi — two teams
3. Sid Gillman — three teams
4. Buddy Ryan — two teams
5. Chuck Knox — three teams
6. Dick Vermeil — two teams
7. George Allen — two teams
8. Weeb Ewbank — two teams
9. Buddy Parker — three teams
10. Hank Stram — two teams

Sec. 07
Row 19
Seat 12
Enter Gate C
Upper Tier

"Here's $20. Bury two."

-Alabama coach Bear Bryant, when asked to contribute $10 to help bury a down-and-out deceased sportswriter

FULL SEASON TICKET

ANSWERS

1. Packers, Chicago Cardinals and Redskins
2. Packers and Redskins
3. L.A. Rams, L.A./San Diego Chargers and Oilers
4. Eagles and Arizona Cardinals
5. L.A. Rams, Bills and Seahawks
6. Eagles and St. Louis Rams
7. L.A. Rams and Redskins
8. Baltimore Colts and Jets
9. Chicago Cardinals, Lions and Steelers
10. Dallas Texans/KC Chiefs and Saints

Sec. 82 Row E Seat 17

Enter Gate B

"I have a lifetime contract. That means I can't be fired during the third quarter if we're ahead and moving the ball."

-Lou Holtz

MOMENTS OF IMMORTALITY

Identify each of these legendary slices of NFL history. They are listed in chronological order with the years provided.

1. "The Greatest Game Ever Played" (1958)
2. "The Sneak" (1967)
3. "The Guarantee" (1969)
4. "The Immaculate Reception" (1972)
5. "The Hail Mary" (1975)
6. "The Catch" (1981)
7. "The Drive" (1986)
8. "The Fumble" (1987)
9. "The Comeback" (1992)
10. "The Music City Miracle" (2000)

ANSWERS

1. The Colts' "Sudden Death" NFL title win over the Giants
2. Bart Starr's three-yard slip into the end zone in the 1967 NFL Championship Game (the "Ice Bowl"), giving the Packers a home victory over the Cowboys
3. Joe Namath's promise that the upstart AFL Jets would beat the heavily favored Colts in the third Super Bowl
4. Franco Harris' shoestring catch of a deflected Terry Bradshaw pass for a touchdown in a 1972 AFC Divisional Playoff game victory over the Raiders in the final seconds.
5. Drew Pearson's catch of a desperation pass by Roger Staubach as the Cowboys beat the Vikings in a playoff game
6. Dwight Clark's reception of a 6-yard Joe Montana pass in the corner of the end zone, putting the 49ers ahead of the Cowboys for good in the 1981 AFC Championship game
7. John Elway's 98-yard march to a game-tying touchdown resulting in an overtime Bronco victory against the Browns in the 1986 AFC Championship Game at Cleveland
8. Ernest Byner's fumble on the 3-yard line, forced and recovered by Jeremiah Castille, ensuring a Broncos victory over the Browns in the 1987 AFC Championship Game
9. Backup quarterback Frank Reich led the Bills from a 35-3 third quarter deficit to an overtime victory over the Oilers in a 1992 AFC Wild Card Game.
10. Frank Wycheck's lateral to Kevin Dyson for a 75-yard kickoff return in a 1999 AFC Wild Card Game with three seconds to go as the Titans beat the Bills

A SIMPLE YES OR NO WILL DO II

1. Are there any NFL teams with nicknames that do not end in "s"?
2. Has a Super Bowl punt return ever resulted in a touchdown?
3. If a field goal attempt is booted through the uprights but then gets blown back through the uprights by a sudden gust of wind, is it still good?
4. Did the USFL win its antitrust suit against the NFL?
5. The first Super Bowl was not a sellout. Were the AFL and NFL championship games both sellouts that season?
6. Did Marvin Gaye ever sing the national anthem at a Super Bowl?
7. Did the Lions and Cowboys ever play each other on Thanksgiving?
8. Did the NFL's first-ever overtime game end with a field goal?
9. Did the 49ers ever play a Super Bowl in a domed stadium?
10. Was Howard Cosell ever part of the TV broadcast team for a Super Bowl?

ANSWERS

1. No
2. No
3. No
4. Yes — The award was one dollar, tripled to three dollars under the antitrust laws.
5. Yes
6. Yes — in Super Bowl V
7. No
8. No — The Colts' Alan Ameche ran for a touchdown on 3rd-and-1 at 8:15 into overtime in the 1958 NFL Championship Game for a 23-17 victory over the Giants.
9. Yes — Super Bowl XVI in the Silverdome in Pontiac and Super Bowl XXIV in the Louisiana Superdome in New Orleans
10. No

FULL SEASON

Sec. 17 Row K Seat 22 Gate F

"When other players started asking me for permission to date my daughter."

-Y.A. Tittle, on when he first thought about retiring

THERE'S A DRAFT IN HERE

1. Name the very first draft choice of the expansion Tampa Bay Bucs, who spent his entire Hall of Fame career with the team.
2. Which NFL team originally drafted John Elway?
3. Which position is most frequently selected number one in the NFL draft?
4. Who was the Pittsburgh Steelers' first-ever draft choice? Was it Charles Dickens, William Shakespeare, William Faulkner or John Grisham?
5. What year did the NFL and AFL first hold a combined draft?
6. The Colts were awarded the Dolphins' 1971 first-round pick by Pete Rozelle in a dispute over coach Don Shula's contract. That choice ended up playing over ten years for the Colts. Who was he?
7. What was unique about defensive tackle Eric Swann, the Cardinal's first-round pick in 1991?
8. Halfback Jay Berwanger was the NFL's first number one draft choice ever (by the Eagles in 1936). What other distinctive "first" did he earn while playing for the University of Chicago?
9. Berwanger never played in the NFL. Who was the first drafted player who did?
10. Which celebrated Oklahoma linebacker did the Seahawks choose as a supplemental pick in 1987, giving up the number one pick in 1988?

ANSWERS

1. Lee Roy Selmon
2. Baltimore Colts
3. Running back
4. Shakespeare, a Notre Dame back
5. 1967
6. Don McCauley
7. He is the only first-round choice with no college experience.
8. The Heisman Trophy
9. Alabama halfback Riley Smith, chosen right after Berwanger by the Boston Redskins
10. Brian Bosworth

Sec. 07
Row 19
Seat 12
Enter
Gate C
Upper Tier

"You usually wind up staying up all night until your best player comes in."

–Former NFL coach John McKay

FULL SEASON TICKET

STADIA

1. Which stadium has been the permanent home of the Pro Bowl since 1980?
2. Due to a blizzard, the first "arena football" game was played in Chicago Stadium, a basketball/hockey arena in 1932 between the Bears and the Portsmouth Spartans. How long was the field?
3. At which facility was Super Bowl I played?
4. Which team's home field was previously known as Sullivan Stadium and Shaefer Stadium?
5. The Bears moved to Soldier Field in 1970. What was their home field before that?
6. Which AFL team and NFL team shared the Cotton Bowl from 1960-62?
7. Which college football stadium was the site of Super Bowl XIX as well as a 1989 49ers home game that moved due to the earthquake?
8. What are the three rivers of Pittsburgh's Three Rivers Stadium?
9. The first Pro Bowl, in 1939, was played at Wrigley Field, but not in Chicago. Explain.
10. Which college stadium, built in 1895 and home to the Eagles from 1958-70, is the oldest football stadium in the country?

ANSWERS

1. Aloha Stadium, Honolulu
2. 80 yards
3. Memorial Coliseum, in Los Angeles
4. The Boston/New England Patriots
5. Wrigley Field
6. The Dallas Texans and the Dallas Cowboys
7. Stanford Stadium in Palo Alto
8. The Allegheny, Monongahela and Ohio
9. Wrigley Field in L.A. was then home to the Cubs' farm team. It was named for the same Wrigley.
10. University of Pennsylvania's Franklin Field

Sec. Row Seat
82 E 17

Enter Gate B

"When I started out I looked like Barry Sanders, and when I finished I looked like Colonel Sanders."

–256-pound lineman Reggie Johnson, after a 34-yard return of a squib kickoff

BY ANY OTHER NAME II

Again, identify each of the following who is not generally known by his given name which is provided in the clues.

1. David is credited with coining the term "sack."
2. Oail (yes, Oail) always wore a hat on the sidelines unless he was coaching in a domed stadium.
3. Norman was fired by ABC after two seasons in the booth on *Monday Night Football*.
4. Elbert never did get to do his "shuffle" in Super Bowl XXIII.
5. William scored the first touchdown in Super Bowl history.
6. Robert overcame wounds sustained in Vietnam and went on to play in four Super Bowls.
7. The Packers drafted Bryan in the 17th round in 1956.
8. Walter moved from the Broncos third string quarterback to John Elway's backup late in the 1997 season, getting into the second half of the final regular season game.
9. John was the intended receiver for the "Immaculate Reception."
10. Bronislaw was a charter inductee into the Hall of Fame.

ANSWERS

1. Deacon Jones
2. Bum Phillips
3. Boomer Esiason
4. Ickey Woods
5. Max McGee
6. Rocky Bleier
7. Bart Starr
8. Bubby Brister
9. Frenchy Fuqua
10. Bronko Nagurski

"I had a Cadillac offered to me a couple of times. You know how that works. They give you the Cadillac one year, and the next year they give you the gas to get out of town."

–Ohio State football coach Woody Hayes

Sec. 16
Row 51
Seat 7a
Enter Gate G
Lower Tier

GRIDIRON TO SILVER SCREEN

1. This 1981 comedy featured both a Beatle and a Raider.
2. Hall of Famers Y.A. Tittle, Dick Butkus and Johnny Unitas all had cameos as "opposing coaches" in this 1999 Oliver Stone movie.
3. Joe Kapp played the "Walking Boss" and Ray Nitschke played Bogdanski in this 1974 guy flick.
4. He left a wildly successful football career for a fairly successful acting career. Among his film credits are *100 Rifles*, *Slaughter* and *El Condor*.
5. This 1970 Oscar-nominated black comedy had roles for Fred Williamson and Ben Davidson.
6. Carl Weathers (Apollo Creed in the *Rocky* movies) was never a pro boxer but did get into eight games as a linebacker for this NFL team.
7. He was a linebacker for the Steelers and the Rams as well as one of the more eloquent movie Tarzans in the '60s.
8. He shared a motorcycle and a bed with Ann-Margret in a 1970 biker flick.
9. Joe Schmidt, Alex Karras and Mike Lucci were among the Detroit Lions playing themselves in this 1968 movie adaptation of a best-selling nonfiction book.
10. Hall of Famer Terry Bradshaw had roles in these three Burt Reynolds movies.

ANSWERS

1. *Caveman*, with Ringo Starr and John Matuszak
2. *Any Given Sunday*
3. *The Longest Yard*
4. Jim Brown
5. *M*A*S*H*
6. Oakland Raiders
7. Mike Henry
8. Joe Namath in *CC and Company*
9. *Paper Lion*
10. *Hooper, The Cannonball Run* and *Smokey and the Bandit II*

FULL SEASON

Sec. 17 Row K Seat 22 Gate F

"I don't like the idea of practicing six days to play one."

–Baseball Hall of Famer Robin Yount, on football

GETTING AROUND

Can you name all the NFL (or AFL) teams each of the following has played for? The number of teams is provided.

1. Eric Dickerson — four teams
2. Deion Sanders — four teams
3. Doug Flutie — three teams
4. Steve DeBerg — six teams
5. Jim Plunkett — three teams
6. Y.A. Tittle — three teams
7. Herschel Walker — four teams
8. George Blanda — four teams
9. Dave Casper — three teams
10. Mike Ditka — three teams

ANSWERS

1. Rams, Colts, Raiders and Falcons
2. Falcons, 49ers, Cowboys and Redskins
3. Bears, Patriots and Bills
4. 49ers, Broncos, Buccaneers, Chiefs, Dolphins and Falcons
5. Patriots, 49ers and Raiders
6. Colts, 49ers and Giants
7. Cowboys, Vikings, Eagles and Giants
8. Bears, Colts, Oilers and Raiders
9. Raiders, Oilers and Vikings
10. Bears, Eagles and Cowboys

"If it's a boy, my neighbors have some friends who want me to name him Bjorn, so the headlines could read, 'BJORN ZORN BORN.'"

–NFL quarterback Jim Zorn, when asked if he had come up with possible names for his child

Sec. 16
Row 51
Seat 7a
Enter Gate G
Lower Tier

DOUBLE DIGITS

Match the following double-digit uniform numbers with the all-time greats who wore them.

1. 00	A. Lee Roy Jordan
2. 11	B. John Riggins
3. 22	C. Jim Otto
4. 33	D. Dan Hampton
5. 44	E. Lynn Swann
6. 55	F. Lyle Alzado
7. 66	G. Ray Nitschke
8. 77	H. Sammy Baugh
9. 88	I. Bobby Layne
10. 99	J. Phil Simms

"I haven't read it yet."

–Baltimore Colts Hall of Famer Johnny Unitas, when asked about his new book

ANSWERS

1. C
2. J
3. I
4. H
5. B
6. A
7. G
8. F
9. E
10. D

FULL SEASON

Sec. 17 Row K Seat 22 Gate F

"If talking was an Olympic sport, Theismann is Jim Thorpe."

–Sportswriter Mike Lupica, about former quarterback turned broadcaster Joe Theismann

WHO 'DAT? II

1. He was a track star for the University of Maryland who spent three seasons as a 49ers wide receiver in the early '80s.
2. This Hall of Famer conducted the very first honorary Super Bowl coin toss.
3. At 45 he was the oldest player to suit up for a Super Bowl.
4. He began his pro career in the USFL but retired as the NFL's all-time leader in sacks.
5. He is in the pro football Hall of Fame as a tackle and the pro baseball Hall of Fame as an umpire.
6. In 1996 he became the NFL's first two-way starter since the early '60s.
7. He was traded from Cleveland to Miami and proceeded to rewrite the Dolphins receiving records.
8. He was the first NFL coach to get soaked in the now traditional "Gatorade dunk."
9. In 1952 this rookie intercepted 14 passes (in a 12-game season), a record that stood at century's end.
10. In the early '50s this Chicago Bear became the NFL's first modern middle linebacker when he dropped back from middle guard on obvious passing plays.

ANSWERS

1. Renaldo Nehemiah
2. Red Grange, for Super Bowl XII — The first 11 were conducted by the officials.
3. Steve DeBerg, in Super Bowl XXXIII
4. Reggie White
5. Cal Hubbard
6. Deion Sanders of the Cowboys — He started all 16 games at cornerback and eight at wide receiver.
7. Paul Warfield
8. Bill Parcells, with the Giants
9. Dick Lane
10. Bill George

Sec. 07
Row 19
Seat 12
Enter Gate C
Upper Tier

"In my next life I want to come back as a kicker, or some fat lady's poodle. It's basically the same."

–Pigskin commentator and former Raider defensive end Howie Long

FULL SEASON TICKET

READ ALL ABOUT IT!

Give the year for each of the following headlines.

1. MONTANA ANNOUNCES RETIREMENT
2. BEARS LEGEND HALAS DIES AT 87
3. BILLS LOSE 4TH CONSECUTIVE SUPER BOWL
4. ALZADO'S COMEBACK FIZZLES — CUT BY RAIDERS AFTER FINAL PRE-SEASON GAME
5. USFL IS OFFICIALLY KAPUT
6. RAIDERS MOVE TO L.A.
7. RAIDERS MOVE BACK TO OAKLAND
8. PETE ROZELLE RETIRES
9. NFL'S PIRATES CHANGE NAME TO "STEELERS"
10. NFL TO FIELD REPLACEMENT PLAYERS

ANSWERS

1. 1995
2. 1983
3. 1994
4. 1990
5. 1986
6. 1982
7. 1995
8. 1989
9. 1940
10. 1987

Sec. 82 Row E Seat 17

Enter Gate B

"Most football players are temperamental. That's 90% temper and 10% mental."

-Former Chicago Bear Doug Plank

THEIR LIFE'S WORK

1. Who is the former Colts receiver who parlayed his $4,864 winner's share check from the 1959 championship game into the Hardee's burger chain and later became the first former NFL player of the modern era to own a team?
2. Former Chargers place-kicker Rolf Benirschke pulled a brief stint as host of which TV game show?
3. Who spent three years in the NFL and 31 years as the ultimate benchwarmer after President Kennedy appointed him to the U.S. Supreme Court?
4. Bears and Vikings Hall of Famer Alan Page is the first black candidate to be elected to statewide office in which state?
5. Which cabinet post did former Bills quarterback Jack Kemp hold in the Bush Administration?
6. Who retired from football at 27 as one of the game's top defensive tackles to pursue a successful career as a Grammy-winning songwriter, with Bonnie Raitt's *I Can't Make You Love Me* among his many hits?
7. Record-holding Seahawks receiver Steve Largent was elected to the Hall of Fame in 1995. What was he elected to in 1994?
8. Who ran the ball for the Vikings, Jets and Seahawks before landing the role of Officer Joe Coffey on Hill Street Blues?
9. Which former NFL great joined Chip Ganassi in 1995 as a partner in the Target/Chip Ganassi racing team?
10. In 1980 the Marriott Corporation purchased the Gino's fast food chain from which two former Colts teammates?

ANSWERS

1. Jerry Richardson, founder/owner of the Carolina Panthers
2. *Wheel of Fortune*
3. Byron White
4. Minnesota (Supreme Court)
5. Secretary of Housing and Urban development (HUD)
6. Mike Reid of the Bengals
7. The U.S. House of Representatives
8. Ed Marinaro
9. Joe Montana
10. Alan Ameche and Gino Marchetti

FULL SEASON

Sec. 17 Row K Seat 22 Gate F

"He's a great player. He ceases to amaze me every day."

-Former Tampa Bay Bucs coach Ray Perkins, about placekicker Gary Anderson

PIGSKIN POTPOURRI

1. The score was 73-0, the largest blowout in NFL history. Who beat whom in that 1940 championship game?
2. Who were the "Steagles"?
3. There have been four head coaches in the first 40 years of the Dallas Cowboys. All have been fired by Jerry Jones. Name the four.
4. In the '40s, Browns owner Arthur McBride gave players cut from the 33-man roster jobs as drivers for his cab company rather than risk losing them to other teams. This gave rise to what still-used term for reserve players?
5. What distinction do Chuck Howley of the Cowboys and Bobby Richardson of baseball's Yankees share regarding championship teams?
6. Which NFL team lost a record 26 consecutive games over two seasons?
7. In 1983 the Cowboys' Tony Dorsett set what record that may someday be tied but will never be broken?
8. How did the Packers win the NFL championship twice in 1967?
9. Which Steelers backup quarterback became the first player to qualify for an NFL pension without playing in a single game?
10. The Steelers won four Super Bowls but many consider their 1976 team the best ever. Which subsequent Super Bowl champ did the injury-riddled team lose the AFC championship to that season?

ANSWERS

1. Bears over Redskins
2. The popular name for the 1943 merger of the Steelers and the Eagles due to the wartime manpower shortage
3. Tom Landry, Jimmy Johnson, Barry Switzer and Chan Gailey
4. "Taxi squad"
5. They were both MVPs for a losing cause — Howley in Super Bowl V and Richardson for the 1960 Yankees.
6. The expansion Tampa Bay Buccaneers of 1976-77
7. Longest run from scrimmage (99 yards)
8. They beat the Cowboys on January 1, 1967 for the 1966 title and beat the same team again on December 31, 1967 for the 1967 title.
9. Cliff Stoudt
10. Oakland Raiders

MONIKERS II

Again, identify the football figures known by each of the following nicknames.

1. Bambi
2. Bulldog
3. L.T.
4. Hacksaw
5. Night Train
6. Broadway Joe
7. Bullet Bill
8. Tippy Toes
9. Skeets
10. Ice Cube

Sec. 07
Row 19
Seat 12
Enter Gate C
Upper Tier

"We gave the interior decorator an unlimited budget and he exceeded it."

-K.C. Chiefs owner Lamar Hunt, about his plush new office

FULL SEASON TICKET

ANSWERS

1. Lance Alworth
2. Clyde Turner
3. Lawrence Taylor
4. Jack Reynolds
5. Dick Lane
6. Joe Namath
7. Bill Dudley
8. Alex Karras
9. Renaldo Nehemiah
10. Gerald McNeil

"Why are we honoring this man? Have we run out of human beings?"

–Milton Berle, roasting former "Monday Night Football" commentator Howard Cosell

Sec. 16

Row 51

Seat 7a

Enter Gate G

Lower Tier

CLOSING IT OUT

What was the final NFL team each of the following played for?

1. Ronnie Lott
2. James Lofton
3. John Mackey
4. Franco Harris
5. John Henry Johnson
6. Art Monk
7. Joe Namath
8. Jim Ringo
9. Johnny Unitas
10. Preston Pearson

Sec. 07
Row 19
Seat 12
Enter Gate C
Upper Tier

"Franco Harris faked me out so bad one time I got a 15-yard penalty for grabbing my own face mask."

-D.D. Lewis

FULL SEASON TICKET

ANSWERS

1. Jets (1994)
2. Eagles (1993)
3. Chargers (1972)
4. Seahawks (1984)
5. Oilers (1966)
6. Eagles (1995)
7. Rams (1977)
8. Eagles (1967)
9. Chargers (1973)
10. Cowboys (1980)

nthe Jaguars
Bowl Bears Ravens
phins Packers Saints Cotton
rgers Jets Bucs Orange Bowl 49ers
s Falcons Fiesta Bowl Cowboys Colts
otton Bowl Browns Raiders Eagles V
e Bowl 49ers Steelers Seahawks Ti
Bowl Cowboys Colts NFL Bengals Pa
ders Eagles Vikings Patriots Super B
eahawks Titans Cardinals Bills Suga
engals Panthers Rose Bowl Giants C
lts Super Bowl Jaguars Rams Redski
r Bowl Bears Ravens NCAA Broncos
hiefs Dolphins Packers Saints Cotton
skins Chargers Jets Bucs Orange Bo
AA Broncos Falcons Fiesta Bowl Cow
Saints Cotton Bowl Browns Raiders
ucs Orange Bowl 49ers Steelers Sea
Fiesta Bowl Cowboys Colts NFL B
Raiders Eagles Vikings Patrio
ks Titans Cardinals
Rose Bowl Ran